Let's Chat!
ESL Dialogues
Intermediate

by
Barbara Agor
Stewart Agor
Martha Hansen

Frank Schaffer
An imprint of Carson-Dellosa Publishing LLC
Greensboro, North Carolina

Authors: Barbara Agor, Stewart Agor, Martha Hansen
Development House: Words & Numbers
Design and Production: Ophelia M. Chambliss

Frank Schaffer
An imprint of Carson-Dellosa Publishing LLC
PO Box 35665
Greensboro, NC 27425 USA

© 2005, Carson-Dellosa Publishing LLC. The purchase of this material entitles the buyer to reproduce worksheets and activities for classroom use only—not for commercial resale. Reproduction of these materials for an entire school or district is prohibited. No part of this book may be reproduced (except as noted above), stored in a retrieval system, or transmitted in any form or by any means (mechanically, electronically, recording, etc.) without the prior written consent of Carson-Dellosa Publishing LLC. Frank Schaffer is an imprint of Carson-Dellosa Publishing LLC.

Printed in the USA • All rights reserved.
4 5 6 7 GLO 13 12 11 10

ISBN 978-0-76823-077-2
232107784

Contents

To the Helper   iv
To the Learner   vi

Chapter 1   Home

1. Good News and Bad News   1
2. Off to School   3
3. First One Thing and Then Another   4
4. I Really Want to Help, But…   6
5. Basketball, Pizza, and True Love   8
6. Are Dreams Important?   10
7. I Got to Play Cinderella!   12
8. What Is A Friend?   14
9. Can You Do Me a Favor?   16
10. I Need Your Help   18
11. Dollars for Dancing   19

Chapter 2   School

1. I Don't Feel Too Good   21
2. Don't Give Up   22
3. Take a Chair   24
4. The Permission Slip   25
5. How Do We Know What's Important?   27
6. Talkin' Trash   29
7. The Principal's Haircut   31
8. Are You Hungry Today?   33
9. Bullies on the Bus   34
10. Making Hypotheses   36
11. Why Do We Call Him "Mr. Claude"?   38
12. Cast Your Vote!   41

Chapter 3   The Wider World

1. Riding a Bike   44
2. Stranger Danger   45
3. Let *Us* Do the Shopping!   46
4. Going to the Mall   49
5. What Size Are You?   51
6. At the Grocer's   53
7. Open Wide!   54
8. Gone Fishing   56
9. What Are Friends For?   59
10. A Visit to the Zoo   61

Chapter 4   Just for Fun

1. Stories of Nasruddin   64
2. Knock-Knock Jokes   66
3. Does He Bite?   68
4. I Can Read Your Mind   69

Language Functions   72

To the Helper

How might a helper use these dialogues with English language learners?

This book contains dialogues at intermediate speaking and reading levels for students of a variety of ages (grades 3-8). Some of these dialogues may be more appropriate for older students than younger. Please read each dialogue before using, and choose those that are most appropriate for the students in your class. Here are some tips for using these dialogues with intermediate students.

1. Allow simple listening. The principal section of each dialogue sequence (marked with an audio CD icon) is recorded on the companion audio CD.

2. Connect listening with understanding. Just listening to meaningless dialogues is not very helpful. Learners at the lower intermediate level may appreciate dialogues that can be illustrated by actions, such as "Off to School" or "Can You Do Me a Favor?"

3. Encourage memorization, but only a little. Grabbing a bit of language, repeating it, and feeling the way it sounds and rolls over the tongue gets language inside the mind and the body. However, there is no need for learners to memorize everything, and forcing them to do so could be counterproductive. Instead, encourage them to pick out the words and phrases that come easily, that have particular meaning for them, or that just sound good. Also help them identify those words, phrases, and sentences that are more difficult, but seem likely to be useful to them as they negotiate their daily lives in a new language. Then let the rest of the dialogue wash over them. They will absorb much more than they realize.

4. Combine reading and speaking. A strategy called "read and look up" provides wonderful support for students who are able to read in English. They select a dialogue or part of a dialogue to recite. They may look at the page as much and as often as they want. However, when they speak, they must look up, and not look at the book. At first, students may only be able to speak a

To the Helper

few words at a time before they need to consult the book again in order to lurch forward with a few more words. Soon they will begin to put words and phrases together in meaningful chunks, and, before they know it, they will manage whole lines.

5. Encourage students to build variations. Some of the dialogues are followed by variations. These variations provide additional practice but also serve as guides to students about how they might further adapt a dialogue.

6. Focus on the story. With their predictable structure of beginning, middle, and end, stories provide a scaffold for understanding. Many of the dialogues in this book can be read as stories, in which the opening dialogue and its continuations pose a problem and work toward a solution. Give learners the opportunity to agree or disagree with the solution in the dialogue. That will lead them to discuss, rethink, rewrite, re-enact, or transform the dialogue in ways that are meaningful to them.

7. Promote transformations of the dialogues. You can also support learners by encouraging them to transform the dialogues into some other form. For students who understand but are not yet comfortable speaking, select some segment of a dialogue and suggest that they pantomime it. For student artists, look for parts of dialogues that they can illustrate. Later, these students or others can rearrange the illustrations, try new sequences, or use the illustrations as prompts to perform parts of the original dialogues.

8. Use the index of language functions. At the end of this book, you will find a listing of language functions that reflect standards established by the international organization TESOL (Teachers of English to Speakers of Other Languages). For easy reference, these functions are indexed to the specific dialogues in which they appear.

Special thanks to Louis Carrillo, Luz M. Aranda, and Ophelia M. Chambliss.

Barbara Agor, Stewart Agor, Martha Hansen

To the Learner

This is your book. We hope that you enjoy it. Here are some tips that we think will help you learn and enjoy learning.

1. You don't have to start at the beginning of the book. Find the dialogues that interest you. Start with ones that are short if you prefer. Or start with long dialogues if they are about something in your life—like solving a problem at home or in school. (The dialogues that are recorded on the audio CD are marked with an audio CD icon in the margin.)

2. When you read or listen to a dialogue, you don't have to understand and remember every single line. Think about it—when you hear people talking, you don't understand every single thing that they say, do you? But some things stick, and you remember them—what they mean and how they sound. These dialogues are no different from real life in this way.

3. When you are reading or listening to a dialogue, you can pay more attention to some parts and less attention to others. How? Use a highlighter to mark a few words or phases that you would like to be able to say easily and naturally. (If you don't own this book, write the words or phrases on a separate piece of paper.)

4. Find people who will read and practice the dialogues with you. Look at the end of each dialogue, where there are questions, thoughts, and ideas for you and others to talk about. You will think of other ways to practice and expand the dialogue. Do them.

5. Finally, don't give up! We hope this book will add to your good days and will be a helpful friend on your journey toward learning English.

Barbara Agor, Stewart Agor, Martha Hansen

HOME

CHAPTER 1

1 Good News and Bad News

Tom and Alexander
On the telephone, Friday night

(Phone rings.)

Tom:	Hello?
Alexander:	Hi, Tom. It's me, Alexander.
Tom:	Hi, Alexander.
Alexander:	I just got a new bike! The same kind as yours.
Tom:	That's great! Do you want to come over on Saturday? We could ride our bikes together.
Alexander:	Yeah, but I have to ask my mother.
Tom:	OK, I'll wait.
Alexander:	She's not here now. But I'll ask when she comes home. Then I'll call you back. OK?
Tom:	OK.
Alexander:	Bye.
Tom:	Bye.

1a (continuation)

(Phone rings.)

Tom:	Hello?
Alexander:	Hi, Tom. It's me.
Tom:	Me, who?
Alexander:	You know who! Alexander!
Tom:	I'm just kidding you.
Alexander:	Oh. My mother says OK.
Tom:	Good!
Alexander:	But she says I can't ride my bike on the road.

Tom: That's OK. We can take our bikes to the school parking lot and ride there.
Alexander: Yeah, that's a good idea. What time?
Tom: What about…one o'clock?
Alexander: That's good. See you then. Bye.
Tom: Bye.

1b (continuation)
Alexander and Dave
On the telephone, Sunday night
(Phone rings.)

Alexander: Hello?
Dave: Hi, Alexander, this is Dave.
Alexander: Hi Dave. What's up?
Dave: Aw, nothin'. What'd you do this weekend?
Alexander: It's a bad story.
Dave: Why? What happened?
Alexander: Well, I got a new bike.
Dave: Yeah…
Alexander: And Tom and I went to the school parking lot to ride it.
Dave: Yeah…
Alexander: And you know that big tree by the parking lot?
Dave: Yeah.
Alexander: Well, I sort of crashed into it.
Dave: Oh no! Are you OK?
Alexander: Yeah, I'm OK, but my bike's a mess.
Dave: What's wrong with it?
Alexander: The front wheel is all bent, and a lot of the spokes are broken.
Dave: Oh that's too bad. How did it happen?
Alexander: Well, Tom and I were racing, and I sort of forgot where the brakes were. Then, bam! Into the tree.
Dave: Too bad, pal. Can you get another bike?
Alexander: Not right away. Maybe sometime.
Dave: That's too bad. Well, see you in school tomorrow.
Alexander: Yeah, bye.

EXPANSION

Write a dialogue in which you and a friend arrange by phone to do something together. Read your dialogue aloud with someone else playing the part of your friend. Read through it a few times. Ask your teacher to listen to your pronunciation.

2 Off to School

Johnny and Mrs. Sands
In the kitchen

Johnny: Bye, Mom!
Mrs. Sands: Whoa! Hold on a minute. Let me look at you to see if you're ready to go.
Johnny: I'm ready.
Mrs. Sands: Blow your nose. It's running.
Johnny: OK. *(sound of nose blowing)*
Mrs. Sands: What about your homework?
Johnny: Oh. It's in my books.
Mrs. Sands: And where are your books?
Johnny: Oops. Uh… Right there on the table. OK, I've got them. *Now* can I go?
Mrs. Sands: Just a minute. What about your lunch bag? Did you take it out of the refrigerator?
Johnny: Oh, yeah. I forgot. All right. There, I've got it.
Mrs. Sands: One more little thing, Johnny. What month is it?
Johnny: Uh… January, isn't it?
Mrs. Sands: That's right! It's freezing outside. Don't you think you should wear your coat?
Johnny: Oh, yeah. Forgot that too.
Mrs. Sands: Arm in the first sleeve. There. Arm in the second sleeve.
Johnny: All set now. Finally! Bye, Mom!
Mrs. Sands: Wait a minute!
Johnny: Oh no! What now?
Mrs. Sands: Blow your nose again.

EXPANSION

You can make this dialogue even longer. What else could Johnny forget? What things do you forget?

3 First One Thing and Then Another

Angelina and Betsy

On the sidewalk, waiting for the school bus

Angelina: Hi, how was your weekend?
Betsy: Well, I guess you could say it was interesting.
Angelina: Why? What happened?
Betsy: You mean, "What didn't happen!"
Angelina: Tell me about it.
Betsy: Well, first it was the cat.
Angelina: Oh, your mean old cat named Ralph?
Betsy: That one. I agree he's mean. But the neighbor's dog is meaner.
Angelina: Oh, yes. I know that dog. He chased me home once.
Betsy: Well, this time the dog chased Ralph the Cat up a tree.
Angelina: Then what did you do?
Betsy: We had no idea. But the neighbor said we should call the Humane Society.
Angelina: And?
Betsy: They came, but Ralph the Cat wouldn't come down.
Angelina: So then what?
Betsy: It worked out. The guy from the Humane Society gave up, but as he left, he told us not to worry.
Angelina: Not to worry?
Betsy: No. He said Ralph the Cat will come down later. And he asked, "How many dead cat skeletons have you seen up in trees?"
Angelina: Pretty funny. So, did Ralph the Cat come down?
Betsy: Yeah, but it took hours. We didn't even see him come down. The next thing we knew, Ralph the Cat was in the kitchen asking for dinner.
Angelina: So it all worked out. But it sounds like you had more troubles on the weekend.

Chapter One: HOME

3a (continuation)

Betsy: Yes, this is a weekend I want to forget.
Angelina: So, tell me more.
Betsy: Well, next it was the hot water heater.
Angelina: The what?
Betsy: That thing in the basement that makes water hot.
Angelina: Oh, yes. We have one.
Betsy: Everyone does. Well, my brother went downstairs to put in the wash, and the floor was covered with water.
Angelina: Then what did you do?
Betsy: We had no idea. But our helpful neighbor heard us yelling and came over.
Angelina: And?
Betsy: He helped us find a sticker on the hot water heater. It had a telephone number.
Angelina: So then what?
Betsy: It worked out. We called the number and the guy from the water heater company came over the same day. He fixed a little thing and said not to worry.
Angelina: Not to worry?
Betsy: No. He said this hot water heater is a good one, and has a lot of years left in it.
Angelina: You were lucky.
Betsy: Well, we didn't feel lucky when it happened. And then, the next disaster...

EXPANSION

What disasters have happened in your house? Pretend that you are Betsy, and tell Angelina about your next disaster.

4 I Really Want to Help, But...

Suzanne and Rob
On the telephone

(Phone rings.)

Suzanne: Hello?
Rob: Hi, Suzanne. How are you doing?
Suzanne: Actually, not great. You know, sometimes family stuff is a problem.
Rob: Sure is.
Suzanne: Like last Friday.
Rob: Last Friday?
Suzanne: Yeah. I had to miss school.
Rob: Oh, yes. You were absent. How come?
Suzanne: My parents had a problem with the gas and electric bill.
Rob: So?
Suzanne: Well, you know their English isn't that great yet.
Rob: Um...hum...like my parents when we first came.
Suzanne: So they had to go downtown to the gas and electric office.
Rob: And I know what else: You had to go with them.
Suzanne: Right. And by the time we took one bus, changed to get the second bus, got lost, and waited an hour in the office...
Rob: Don't tell me. I know. School was over.
Suzanne: You got it. I really want to help my family, but I wish there were an easier way.

4a (variation)

Suzanne: Hello?
Rob: Hi, Suzanne. How are you doing?
Suzanne: Actually, not great. You know, sometimes family stuff is a problem.
Rob: Sure is.
Suzanne: Like last Friday.
Rob: Last Friday?
Suzanne: Yeah. I had to miss school.

Chapter One: HOME

Rob: Oh, yes. You were absent. How come?
Suzanne: My little brother had a fever.
Rob: So?
Suzanne: Well, you know my parents' English isn't that great yet.
Rob: Um…hum…like my parents when we first came.
Suzanne: So they had to take my brother to the doctor.
Rob: And I know what else: You had to go with them.
Suzanne: Right. And by the time we took one bus, changed to get the second bus, got lost, and waited an hour in the doctor's office…
Rob: Don't tell me. I know. School was over.
Suzanne: You got it. I really want to help my family, but I wish there were an easier way.

4b (continuation)
On the telephone, the next day

Suzanne: Hello?
Rob: Hi, Suz. It's Rob.
Suzanne: Oh, hi, Rob. What's up?
Rob: You know, I've been thinking…
Suzanne: About my family…and missing school.
Rob: Yeah. And I have an idea. Let's talk to your counselor.
Suzanne: My counselor?
Rob: Sure, they help students with problems.
Suzanne: And I definitely have a problem.
Rob: Good. Tomorrow, then?
Suzanne: But wait a minute… It's family business. Shouldn't that be private?
Rob: Counselors are special. They keep things private.

EXPANSION

Sometimes children have to take responsibility in the family because they speak the most English. Tell about a time when you helped your family. Can you think of a way that Suzanne could have helped her family without missing school?

5 Basketball, Pizza, and True Love

Peter and Mrs. Anders

In the living room

Peter: Hi, Mom. Are you still up?

Mrs. Anders: Yes. I like to wait until I see that you are home safe. Did you have a good time at the game?

Peter: Yeah! It was really exciting.

Mrs. Anders: What did you do afterwards?

Peter: Sarah's father took five of us out for pizza. And I bought Sarah a soda.

Mrs. Anders: Oh? And why did you do that?

Peter: I…well, uh…because…because it was her father who gave us a ride.

Mrs. Anders: I see. Well, it sounds like you had a good time. Now, go to bed and get some sleep.

5a (continuation)

Peter and Janina

On the telephone, the next evening

Peter: Hi, Janina. It's Peter.

Janina: Hi, Peter. What are you doing?

Peter: I wanted to tell you about the game last night. I went with Sarah and her friends.

Janina: So what happened?

Peter: The game was great. It was tied and they had to play overtime. Everybody was excited. I was sitting right next to Sarah, and she cheered so loud she almost broke my eardrum!

Janina: Sarah, eh? But what about the game? How did it end?

Peter: Oh, yeah. We won by one basket.

Janina: Great!

Peter: Then afterward, Sarah's father drove us all to get some pizza. To celebrate. We had a really great time.

Janina: I wish I had been there.

Peter: Yeah. Me too.

Chapter One: HOME

Janina: Well, I've got to do some homework.

Peter: Before you hang up, uh… You're good friends with Sarah, right?

Janina: Oh yes, we're very good friends.

Peter: Well, I was wondering if—maybe tomorrow in school—if, um—if you could find out if she had a good time last night.

Janina: Peter! You wouldn't be in love or anything, now, would you?

Peter: Oh no! No. Nothing like that. I'm just a little—you know—curious.

Janina: I see. Well, I think I could talk to her.

Peter: *(excited)* You could!

Janina: Yes. As a matter of fact, she called me tonight.

Peter: She did? Did she say anything about me—I mean, about the game?

Janina: She didn't mention the game, but she did want me to try to find something out.

Peter: What?

Janina: Well… I don't know if I should say…

Peter: Janina!

Janina: OK. She wanted me to find out whether you had a good time.

Peter: She did?

Janina: Yup. So I guess I'll tell her that you did have a good time, but you're *not* in love with her. Right?

Peter: No! Don't say that! Janina, you're making fun of me, aren't you?

Janina: Sorry. I couldn't resist. But don't worry. I'll play it cool.

Peter: OK. That's good. This is all good. Thanks, Janina!

EXPANSION

Talk about Peter, Sarah, and Janina with other students. What clues did you get that Peter liked Sarah? Why does Peter say he is not in love with Sarah? Why does Janina make fun of Peter?

6 Are Dreams Important?

Priscilla and Miriam
On the telephone

(Phone rings.)

Miriam: Hello?
Priscilla: Hi. It's me. Priscilla.
Miriam: Oh, hi, Priscilla. What's up?
Priscilla: I had the strangest dream last night.
Miriam: Really?
Priscilla: I dreamt I was falling and couldn't grab anything to stop.
Miriam: Did you hit the ground?
Priscilla: No, but I woke up feeling a little startled. Have you ever had a strange dream?
Miriam: No, I never dream.
Priscilla: That's impossible! Everyone dreams!
Miriam: Well, maybe some really short dreams, but then I wake up.

6a (continuation)
Priscilla and Dora

(Phone rings.)

Dora: Hello?
Priscilla: Hi. It's me. Priscilla.
Dora: Oh, hi, Priscilla. What's up?
Priscilla: Dora, have you ever dreamt the same dream over and over?
Dora: Yes. I often dream I'm in the middle of taking a science test.
Priscilla: What happens?
Dora: I never know, but I know when I'm awake, I hate taking science tests.
Priscilla: Are you good in science?
Dora: Science, yes; taking science *tests*, forget about it!
Priscilla: I think you need to figure out why you don't do well on the tests.

6b (continuation)

Priscilla and Sally

(Phone rings.)

Sally: Hello?

Priscilla: Hi. It's me. Priscilla.

Sally: Oh, hi, Priscilla. What's up?

Priscilla: Guess what I dreamt about last night, Sally?

Sally: Winning a million dollars!

Priscilla: Seriously! I dreamt I met the Queen of England.

Sally: OK, why were you thinking of her?

Priscilla: I didn't know at first. But my family and I are planning a trip to London. Now that I think about it, that might have something to do with it.

EXPANSION

Do you remember any of your dreams? Are your dreams long or short? Happy or sad? Tell a friend about your dreams, and try to see if you can figure out any of the reasons behind your dreams.

7 I Got to Play Cinderella!

Eva and Mrs. Hofmeyer
In their apartment

Eva:	*(running into the room, excited)* Mom! Guess what! I got to play Cinderella in school today!
Mrs. Hofmeyer:	How could you do that? What about your accent? How could you pronounce all the English words?
Eva:	I didn't have to speak any English.
Mrs. Hofmeyer:	But how could you play Cinderella without speaking any English?
Eva:	It was a… Oh, what did Mrs. Kornblum say it was? I know! A pant-o-mime. Yeah, that's it. A pantomime.
Mrs. Hofmeyer:	What's a pantomime?
Eva:	Well, it's where you do all the actions, but you don't say any words. And I was Cinderella!
Mrs. Hofmeyer:	A pantomime. How did you know what actions to do?
Eva:	Mrs. Kornblum told us everything we had to do, and if we didn't understand, she showed us.
Mrs. Hofmeyer:	So what did she show you to do?
Eva:	She told me to sit by the fireplace (that's a new word for me—*fireplace*), and then she showed me what to do, and then I sat by the fireplace.
Mrs. Hofmeyer:	You have a fireplace in your classroom?
Eva:	An imaginary one. Everything is imaginary.
Mrs. Hofmeyer:	Oh. What happened then?
Eva:	Well, my mean stepmother—not like you, Mom—and my mean stepsisters got an invitation to the ball. But I couldn't go because they made me stay and sweep the floor.
Mrs. Hofmeyer:	Mean people.
Eva:	Yes, and ugly, too. But not me. I was beautiful.

7a (continuation)

Mrs. Hofmeyer:	This sounds like something I know. That's like a story from our country!
Eva:	Yes but in the end, my fairy godmother came. She had a magic wand, and she gave me a beautiful gown.
Mrs. Hofmeyer:	But not a real gown, right?

Chapter One: HOME

Eva:	No, everything was imaginary.
Mrs. Hofmeyer:	Then what?
Eva:	Then I went to the ball and danced with the prince! Oscar was the prince.
Mrs. Hofmeyer:	And I think I know what happened after that. Did you lose a shoe?
Eva:	Yup. I lost a glass slipper, and when the prince came to see who it fit, my two stepsisters couldn't get their big fat feet into it.
Mrs. Hofmeyer:	But you could, right?
Eva:	Yup, and then the prince and I were married and we lived happily ever after.
Mrs. Hofmeyer:	Happily ever after. How nice. Did you learn many new words?
Eva:	Yeah! I learned a lot of new words, but it was easy. And mostly, it was fun. And Mrs. Kornblum said I did a very good job!

EXPANSION

Tell someone in your family about something you did well at school, something you are proud of. Write a few things that you might say to them.

8 What Is A Friend?

Patricia and Britney
At Patricia's house

Patricia: I am so mad at Sarah. I never want to talk to her again.
Britney: How come? I thought she was your best friend.
Patricia: Not anymore.
Britney: What happened?
Patricia: She wrote a note saying bad things about me.
Britney: A note?
Patricia: Yes, to Maria. Now, Maria, *she's* a good friend.
Britney: What do you mean—a good friend?
Patricia: A good friend cares about your feelings and wouldn't say bad things about you to someone else.
Britney: I agree, but…
Patricia: If Maria cared about your feelings, maybe she shouldn't have mentioned the note.
Britney: Well, I think you want a good friend to be honest and tell you the truth.
Patricia: Even if it hurts?
Britney: Even if it hurts.

8a (variation)

Jorge and Luis
At Jorge's house

Jorge: I'm so mad at Mike. I never want to talk to him again.
Luis: How come? I thought he was your best friend.
Jorge: Not anymore.
Luis: What happened?
Jorge: He invited Jennifer to the party on Saturday.
Luis: Did she say yes?
Jorge: Yeah, but it was the way he told me. He knows that I like Jennifer. He didn't care about my feelings at all. Now you—you're a good friend.
Luis: Sure, I am.
Jorge: A good friend cares about your feelings and wouldn't do something to hurt you.
Luis: I agree, but…

Jorge:	But what?
Luis:	Maybe he didn't know that you like Jennifer.
Jorge:	He knows, trust me. He knows.
Luis:	Do you think you can still be friends?
Jorge:	I don't think so, unless he apologizes to me.
Luis:	What about Jennifer?
Jorge:	I don't know what to do about that. I think maybe I should forget about her.

EXPANSION

Write down three things that you think are important qualities of a friend. Ask a friend to do the same thing. Compare your lists and talk about them.

9 Can You Do Me a Favor?

Pedro and Mischa

At Mischa's house

Mischa: Hi, Pedro. Glad you could come over. I have a favor to ask.
Pedro: Sure, what is it?
Mischa: I want to rearrange my room and I can't do it alone.
Pedro: Fine. I'm feeling strong. Let's get going. What's first?
Mischa: Let's move the desk out of the way, and then we can move the bed where the desk was.
Pedro: OK. You take this end of the desk, and I'll take the other.
Mischa: Be careful when you back up!
Pedro: Ouch! Who put that door there?
Mischa: I said to be careful!
Pedro: It's OK. Now the bed. This time you be the one to walk backwards.
Mischa: Sure. Slowly…slowly…gently. *(a loud thud as the bed hits the floor)*
Pedro: Oops. Did you say "gently"?
Mischa: That's all right. Right where we wanted it.
Pedro: Now what?
Mischa: Let's put the desk under the window.
Pedro: OK. Just push. Ready? Ooomph!
Mischa: That was easy. Now the bookshelf goes near the door and the CD player goes next to the bed.
Pedro: Done. It looks good now. What are you doing with those things?
Mischa: That's junk! I'd better get a box and throw them out.
Pedro: Don't throw them out yet! Can I have those video games?
Mischa: Of course! I really appreciate your helping me today.
Pedro: Any time. In fact, I think my room could use some rearranging. What are you doing after school tomorrow?

EXPANSION

Describe your bedroom. If you could do anything you wanted to it, what would you do?

9a (continuation)
At Pedro's house

Pedro:	Thanks for coming over Mischa!
Mischa:	My pleasure! I owe you one from yesterday, you know.
Pedro:	How do you think I should rearrange my room?
Mischa:	Well, let's see. Whoa! Your bed looks heavier than mine!
Pedro:	Maybe we should leave it where it is.
Mischa:	Oh, no. We can move it! We're super strong! How about over there?
Pedro:	OK, let's try it. Ready? One…two…three…lift!
Mischa:	Ooomph!
Pedro:	Again!
Mischa:	Ooomph!
Pedro:	Once more and we'll have it!
Mischa:	Oooooooooooomph!
Pedro:	There! Perfect!
Mischa:	You know what, Pedro?
Pedro:	What?
Mischa:	I think it looked better where it was!

10 I Need Your Help

Shana and Adrienne
At Shana's house

Shana: Hi, Adrienne. Glad you could come over. Can you do me a favor?

Adrienne: Sure, what is it?

Shana: I don't get the math assignment.

Adrienne: It is tough, but I think I got it. I'll try to help. What's the problem?

Shana: Well, I didn't get much of the lesson. And now I don't know where to start on the homework.

Adrienne: Whenever I feel like that, I depend on the examples. I try to understand those. That usually helps me do the rest.

Shana: Good idea. I usually ignore the examples and get right to the first problem.

Adrienne: OK. Take a look at this example and tell me what you think.

Shana: Hmmm… *(pause)* OK. You subtract seven from the left, and do the same thing on the right.

Adrienne: Right. Whatever you do on the left side of the equal sign, you do the same thing on the right.

Shana: Got it. I wish we had more than one example, though.

Adrienne: I think you understand. Go ahead and start the problems.

Shana: *(talking to herself)* Add 15 to the left. Add 15 to the right. *(louder)* This is making sense. Thanks, Adrienne. You're a great teacher!

EXPANSION

When you are confused in class or confused about homework, what do you do? Ask others what they do too.

Chapter One: HOME

11 Dollars for Dancing

Guillermo and Mrs. Lopez
In the kitchen of their house

Mrs. Lopez: Hi, son. Here, have a cookie.
Guillermo: Thanks, Mom.
Mrs. Lopez: So, how was school today?
Guillermo: OK.
Mrs. Lopez: You don't sound like it was OK. Have another cookie and tell me.
Guillermo: Oh, never mind.
Mrs. Lopez: Guillermo, tell me! You can tell me. I'm your mother.
Guillermo: Well, tomorrow's Saturday, and I wanted to go to the dance at school.
Mrs. Lopez: Yes…
Guillermo: But it costs five dollars. And I'm broke.
Mrs. Lopez: Broke? What happened to your allowance?
Guillermo: Well, I guess I—um—spent it.
Mrs. Lopez: You *guess* you spent it? You don't *know* if you spent it or not?
Guillermo: OK. I spent it. I knew you'd get mad at me.
Mrs. Lopez: Who's mad?
Guillermo: Actually, I was wondering if—if you could lend me five dollars.
Mrs. Lopez: *Lend?* Does that mean you plan to pay me back?
Guillermo: Of course! I… Well, maybe you could just *give* me the five dollars? Because I'm such a sweet boy?
Mrs. Lopez: Do I look like I'm made of money!
Guillermo: No, Mom. But I have an idea. Maybe you could sort of hire me to do some job for you.
Mrs. Lopez: A job? Hmm…a five-dollar job. Well, I've been thinking that the windows could use a good washing.
Guillermo: Great! I'll wash the windows.
Mrs. Lopez: But that's only a three-dollar job.
Guillermo: Oh, Mom!
Mrs. Lopez: But the kitchen floor also needs scrubbing.
Guillermo: A two-dollar job maybe?
Mrs. Lopez: How did you know?

Let's Chat: ESL Dialogues

Guillermo: It's a deal!
Mrs. Lopez: But they've got to be done tomorrow! *Before* you go to the dance.
Guillermo: You got it! Thanks Mom! You're a peach! *(sound of a big, slurpy kiss)*
Mrs. Lopez: Oh!

EXPANSION

Does your family give you money for helping around the house? Make a list of all the jobs you do (or that you could do).

SCHOOL

1 I Don't Feel Too Good

Van and Brian (friends)
In the hallway, after school

Van: Achoo!
Brian: What's wrong?
Van: I don't feel well. I think I have a cold.
Brian: Does that mean you can't sleep over at my house tonight?
Van: Probably not. I'm constantly blowing my nose.
Brian: Gross! Here's the tissue box.
Van: Thanks. *(pause)* Ick! It's all yellow and green.
Brian: Sounds like an infection. You'd better see a doctor.
Van: Good idea.

1a (variation)

Marina and Ms. Stenner
In Mrs. Stenner's classroom

Marina: Ms. Stenner, I need to go to the nurse.
Ms. Stenner: What's wrong? Is it something that can wait?
Marina: I don't think I can take another minute of itching. My arms and legs are all red.
Ms. Stenner: Ooooh! That looks like poison ivy. Here, take this pass to the nurse.
Marina: OK. Thanks.
Ms. Stenner: And don't touch your eyes. Poison ivy is contagious.
Marina: I won't. But it sure itches.

EXPANSION

Have you ever been sick in school? Did you tell your teacher? What happened?

2 Don't Give Up

Luisa and Cristina
In the hallway

Luisa: Cristina, why are you crying?
Cristina: Haven't you heard?
Luisa: Heard what? I just had P.E. class.
Cristina: You know I was trying out for the school play. I sang a song and read something.
Luisa: How did you do?
Cristina: I thought I did really well. I sang my favorite Mexican song, and I thought my English was pretty good for the reading.
Luisa: So what happened?
Cristina: I didn't get the part.
Luisa: Who got it?
Cristina: Emily. They probably liked her better because she didn't have an accent. I'll never try out for anything again.
Luisa: Next time, you might get the part. You're good! Don't give up!

2a (continuation)

Cristina and Mrs. Gray
Later, in the same hallway

Mrs. Gray: Hi, Cristina. Are you OK?
Cristina: Not really, Mrs. Gray.
Mrs. Gray: What's wrong?
Cristina: You know I was trying out for the school play. I sang a song and read something.
Mrs. Gray: How did you do?
Cristina: I thought I did really well. I sang my favorite Mexican song and I thought my English was pretty good for the reading.
Mrs. Gray: So what happened?
Cristina: I didn't get the part.

Let's Chat: ESL Dialogues

Mrs. Gray: Who got it?

Cristina: Emily. They probably liked her better because she didn't have an accent. I'll never try out for anything again.

Mrs. Gray: Well, I'm not sure that's the reason. You know, Emily tried out last year and didn't get a part.

Cristina: She did?

Mrs. Gray: She did. But she kept trying. Next time, you might get the part. You're good! Don't give up!

EXPANSION

Talk with your friends about times when you or they did not succeed but kept trying and eventually succeeded. How does it feel when you don't succeed? How does it feel when you do?

Maria and Mrs. Henley
In Mrs. Henley's classroom, after school

(Maria comes into the class, crying.)

Mrs. Henley: Maria, what's the matter?

Maria: I don't understand my teachers!

Mrs. Henley: Why not? What happened?

Maria: I went into Mr. Garcia's class, and he said "take a chair."

Mrs. Henley: But, what's the problem?

Maria: He got mad at me.

Mrs. Henley: Why did he get mad at you?

Maria: I don't know! I stood there, and he kept saying, "take a chair." And he yelled at me!

Mrs. Henley: Why didn't you take a chair?

Maria: I looked at all the chairs, and they looked OK where they were! I didn't know where else to take one!

Mrs. Henley: Oh, Maria! I see what happened. Mr. Garcia meant for you to sit down. "Take a chair" is another way to say sit down. It doesn't really mean to take it anywhere.

Maria: Oh, now I feel so stupid.

Mrs. Henley: No Maria, you're not the problem. English is the problem. It can be very confusing!

Maria: Thank you, Mrs. Henley. You make me feel better.

Mrs. Henley: I'll talk to Mr. Garcia. He'll understand. Now, dry your tears. And sit d—, uh, take a chair! *(Maria smiles and sits down.)*

EXPANSION

Do you remember something that you didn't understand? Retell this story with your own misunderstanding. If you can't think of any misunderstandings, think about this one: "Gimme five." Did you ever wonder, "Five what?"

4 The Permission Slip

Diego, Thomas, and Mr. Silvan
In Mr. Silvan's class

Mr. Silvan: Class, take home these permission slips for the field trip Friday, and have your parents read and sign them.
Thomas: *(softly)* I'll take it home, but nobody there can read it.
Diego: Yeah, I know what you mean. Whenever we get bills in the mail or important papers from school, it's a problem.
Thomas: What do you do?
Diego: My older sister has to translate them for my parents. She helps them write checks, too.
Thomas: Will she tell them what these field trip papers say?
Diego: No, she can't because she left with my mother for Puerto Rico last week.
Thomas: So how will your father know what they say?
Diego: I'll try to tell him, but sometimes I don't understand everything on the papers. I might not be able to go on the trip.
Thomas: So we both have a problem, don't we?

4a (continuation)
Walking toward Mr. Silvan's classroom

Thomas: I'm all set for the field trip. How about you?
Diego: All set! But it wasn't easy!
Thomas: What happened?
Diego: I tried to remember what Mr. Silvan said in class, and I looked for those words.
Thomas: Like what?
Diego: Well, like the date and the money.
Thomas: Good idea. Did you bring the five dollars?
Diego: Yes. That was easy to understand, because it's a number.
Thomas: Good point.
Diego: There's one thing I didn't get, though.
Thomas: What's that?
Diego: Do you know what a brown bag lunch is? At home, we only have plastic bags. And they're not brown.

EXPANSION

Do you know any students who have had to help their parents understand English? What problems have they encountered? How do they feel about it?

4b (continuation)

In Mr. Silvan's class

Mr. Silvan: Good morning, class! Do you know what tomorrow is?
Class: It's Friday!
Mr. Silvan: And what happens on Friday?
Class: We go on our field trip!
Mr. Silvan: Very good! Now, hand in your permission slips.
Diego: (raising his hand) Mr. Silvan? Thomas and I have a question.
Mr. Silvan: What's your question?
Thomas: Well, it says to bring a "brown bag lunch"…
Diego: But all we have are plastic bags…
Thomas: And they're not brown!
Mr. Silvan: Ha! I should have known "brown bag" might be confusing.
Diego: Why do they say it like that?
Mr. Silvan: It's an old expression. It must have started before we had plastic bags.
Thomas: So will plastic bags be all right?
Mr. Silvan: Of course! I'm going to use a plastic bag myself!

Chapter Two: SCHOOL

5 How Do We Know What's Important?

Marcus, Eliza, Julie, and Mr. Dolan
Mr. Dolan's social studies class

Mr. Dolan: OK, class. For this next assignment, I want you to read the passage on page 63 of our textbook, and make a list of the things that are important. Does anyone have any questions? *(silence)*

Mr. Dolan: No questions? OK, somebody tell *me* what you have to do, so I'll know you understand. Julie?

Julie: We have to read on page 63.

Mr. Dolan: Good! What else? Eliza?

Eliza: Um. Make a list?

Mr. Dolan: Right. What goes on the list? Marcus?

Marcus: Uh… Things… I don't remember. And how will we know what's important?

Mr. Dolan: Good question, Marcus. The way to tell what is important is to ask the passage some questions.

Eliza: We talk to a passage?

Mr. Dolan: Exactly! And most of the best questions to ask start with *wh*. That makes them easy to remember.

Julie: What are those questions?

Mr. Dolan: You just asked one, Julie! You started your question with *what*.

Julie: Oh, yeah! I did, didn't I?

Mr. Dolan: Here are five *wh* words to ask your passage: *who, what, where, when,* and *why.* Can you remember those? Write them down right now, and keep them near you when you read.

(pause, as students write) Now, work in small groups and ask page 63 the *wh* questions.

5a (continuation)

Julie, Marcus, and Eliza

Eliza: Julie, you be the leader. Tell us what to do first.

Julie: OK. First, let's answer the question *what*. What is the passage about?

Marcus: The Civil War.
Julie: Right. Let's write that down. Now *who*. Who fought in the war?
Eliza: Americans.
Julie: Good. Which Americans?
Eliza: Northerners against Southerners.
Marcus: Brothers against brothers.
Julie: Good. *Where*?
Eliza: Umm… It doesn't really say, but I guess all over the country. Where else would they fight—China?
Marcus: Good point.
Julie: When?
Marcus: That's easy. 1861. It says so right in the beginning.
Julie: OK, but what else can we say about when?
Eliza: It lasted for four years.
Marcus: And ended in 1865.
Julie: Finally, *why*? Why did they fight the war?
Marcus: That's usually the hard part.
Eliza: But it's easy this time, because they tell you.
Julie: Right. One of the reasons was slavery. The South was for it, and the North was against it.
Marcus: Another was… Let me see… "States' rights." I don't know exactly what that means.
Julie: Me neither. Maybe we should ask Mr. Dolan later.
Eliza: Yeah.
Julie: OK. We're done!

EXPANSION

Mr. Dolan didn't mention another question word—*how*—because it doesn't start with *wh*. Would you add *how* to your list? How do you and your friends figure out what is important in textbooks you use in other classes? Talk with others to see if you can learn any techniques that will be useful to you.

Chapter Two: SCHOOL

6 Talkin' Trash

Gary and Darren (older students, captains of opposing softball teams), Vladimir and Leo (younger students in a different P.E. class)

In the locker room

Gary: Your team's going down today, Darren.

Darren: We must not be playing you then, Gary. You couldn't beat a colony of ants.

Gary: You guys are about as strong as ants. About as good lookin', too.

Darren: And we could still beat you with one hand tied behind our backs. You've got no pitching, no fielding, no hitting.

Gary: And no chance of losing to a bunch of ants. We're gonna have you for lunch.

Darren: No wonder you never win! You eat ants for lunch. You probably eat termites for dinner too! What do you eat for breakfast, spiders?

Gary: Very funny. What do you mean we never win? We beat you the last time we played!

Darren: That didn't count. Our pitcher was sick.

Gary: That's no excuse! Your team stinks to high heaven! So do you!

Darren: Yeah, and we still whip you. Every time! Because you're a bunch of mud-soaked, rag-tag wussies that don't know a bat from a banana!

(Gary and Darren leave.)

Vladimir: Did you hear them?

Leo: Yeah, they're really mad at each other.

Vladimir: I didn't understand everything they said, did you?

Leo: No. Do they really eat spiders for breakfast?

Vladimir: Do you think they're going to fight?

Leo: Maybe we should tell our teacher, Mr. Borriello.

6a (continuation)
Mr. Borriello, Vladimir, and Leo
Outside on the field

Mr. Borriello: Hi, boys. How's English class coming?

Vladimir: We're learning a lot. *(pause)* Mr. Borriello?

Mr. Borriello: What?

Leo: We were in the locker room, and we think there's going to be a fight.

Mr. Borriello: What did you hear?

Vladimir: You see those two guys across the field?

Mr. Borriello: Yeah, the two big guys, Darren and Gary.

Leo: They were saying mean things to each other.

Vladimir: Like they said, "You stink, and you eat ants."

Leo: And spiders.

Vladimir: And they called each other bad names.

Mr. Borriello: *(laughing)* Well, those are pretty strong words. But I don't think they're going to fight.

Leo: Huh? They sounded really mad.

Vladimir: Like they hate each other.

Mr. Borriello: Actually, they're best friends.

Leo: Why do they talk so mean if they're best friends?

Mr. Borriello: That's called *talkin' trash*, Leo. Sometimes the same words can be mean or friendly, depending on who's saying them and who's hearing them.

Vladimir: English is so confusing. What do you mean?

Mr. Borriello: Well, if you're good friends, talking trash is like arm wrestling. You do it for fun, not to be mean.

Leo: What if you're not good friends?

Mr. Borriello: It would be mean to say it to someone you didn't like or even to a stranger. Then you might really start a fight.

Vladimir: I get it. If you like somebody, you say nasty things to him. If you don't like him, you say nice things. That's English. Everything is backward and upside down and crazy!

Mr. Borriello: Hey! Are you talking trash about my language?

Vladimir: Oops! I guess I was. But we're friends... Right?

EXPANSION

Is there something like "trash talk" in other languages that you know? Tell your friends about it, and ask them if they have examples in their languages.

7 The Principal's Haircut

Mr. Snyder (principal), Sergei, and Julie

At school in homeroom, morning announcements

Mr. Snyder: *(over P.A.)*...and I know that our soccer team has been having a rough year. Now, today is the biggest game of the season. It seems to me that what our team needs is a little extra incentive. So I want everybody to be out there on the bleachers today at 4 P.M...

Sergei: Julie, what's Mr. Snyder saying?

Julie: Shhh. Something about today's game. Listen.

Mr. Snyder: ...and I want you all to cheer your hearts out for our team!

Julie: He wants us to go and cheer.

Mr. Snyder: ...*if* you cheer loud enough, and *if* we win today, then there will be an assembly for the whole school tomorrow at 10 A.M.

Sergei: Oh, good! We miss math!

Julie: Shhh!

Mr. Snyder: ...and Mr. Kelly, the team coach, will shave all the hair off my head!

Sergei: What did he say?

Julie: I think he said he's going to shave his head.

Sergei: What's he going to do that for?

Julie: So we'll win.

Sergei: How will that help us win? Especially if he doesn't do it until tomorrow!

Julie: I guess we'll just have to wait and see.

7a (continuation)

Mr. Snyder, Mr. Dan Kelly, Sergei, Julie, and other students

The next day. At the assembly

Mr. Snyder: Well, Dan, you did it! You beat Lakeland.

Mr. Kelly: Yes we did, Mr. Snyder. Yesterday we trimmed Lakeland, and today we're going to *trim* you!

Sergei: Julie! What does *trim* mean?

Julie: It means give a haircut. Listen.

Mr. Snyder: I hope you know what you're doing, Dan.

Mr. Kelly:	Sorry, Mr. Snyder. I've never shaved a head in my life. Never even gave a haircut. But...a bargain is a bargain!
Students:	*(shouting)* Shave it off! Shave it off! Shave it off!
Julie:	Look! He's starting to shave Mr. Snyder's hair!
Students:	Shave it off! Shave it off!
Sergei:	Oh my gosh! Mr. Snyder's getting bald!
Julie:	Everybody's cheering!
Sergei:	Not Mr. Snyder. He's starting to look weird!
Julie:	He looks so different!
Sergei:	Why doesn't he just go to a real barber?
Julie:	That's not the idea. He's doing it to build school spirit.
Sergei:	Do you really think that helped us win yesterday?
Julie:	Sure. Everybody came out to cheer because they wanted to see Mr. Snyder have his head shaved. And all the cheering helped the team.
Sergei:	This would never happen in another country. Land of the crazy principals!
Julie:	Look! They're finished. Mr. Snyder is bald!
Mr. Snyder:	Well thank you Dan! I don't think you missed a hair. And thanks to all the students who came out and cheered yesterday!
Students:	Yaayy, Mr. Snyder!
Mr. Kelly:	You know, Mr. Snyder, we have another game on Thursday. Shall we do this again?
Mr. Snyder:	I can't, Dan! I don't have any more hair left to shave!

EXPANSION

Do you think Mr. Snyder is a good principal or a bad principal? Why?

Chapter Two: SCHOOL

8 Are You Hungry Today?

Anna and Mrs. Kauffman (a cafeteria worker)
In the school cafeteria

Mrs. Kauffman: Hi there, young lady. What's your name?
Anna: *(slowly)* My name is Anna.
Mrs. Kauffman: And I'm Mrs. Kauffman. Are you hungry today?
(silence)
Mrs. Kauffman: You're new in school, aren't you?
(more silence)
Mrs. Kauffman: Here. I'll help you pick your lunch. I'll point and say the word. Then you tell me yes or no. OK?
Anna: OK.
Mrs. Kauffman: You need to choose one: Either spaghetti…that's this right here. Or chicken nuggets…here. Or tuna salad. Which one? Spaghetti, chicken nuggets, or tuna salad? You can point to what you want.
Anna: Spaghetti. This one.
Mrs. Kauffman: Spaghetti it is! I can see you're a fast learner! Now, you can choose three of all these: side salad…here; green peas…right there; potatoes…here; peaches…here; cake…right here; and a chocolate chip cookie…right there.
Anna: May I have…salad?
Mrs. Kauffman: Yes, you may! And what else? You can choose two more.
Anna: Um…tato… What is that called? Right here.
Mrs. Kauffman: Potatoes. Would you like that?
Anna: Yes.
Mrs. Kauffman: And one more.
Anna: Maybe a cookie.
Mrs. Kauffman: There you are! You can also have milk. Would you like regular…here? Or chocolate… This one here.
Anna: I think… regular. That one.
Mrs. Kauffman: There you go! It's nice to meet you, Anna! Come see me again tomorrow.
Anna: Thank you Mrs. Kaf… Mrs. Koff…
Mrs. Kauffman: Kauffman.
Anna: Thank you, Mrs. Kauffman.
Mrs. Kauffman: You're welcome, Anna.

EXPANSION

Think about someone who helped you when you were first learning English. Write them a letter telling you what you remember, and how it helped. If you can find that person, give it to him or her.

9 Bullies on the Bus

Marta, Mrs. Rose Vanek, and Mr. Peter Vanek
Vanek living room

Mrs. Vanek: Hello, dear, How was school today?

Marta: *(pause)* Mom, when you were in school, were kids mean to each other?

Mrs. Vanek: Mean…like how?

Marta: Well, on the bus. Did they pick on each other?

Mrs. Vanek: Children are often mean. It's part of growing up.

Mr. Vanek: What's going on, Marta?

Marta: On our bus, these two boys who always sit together… They pick on smaller kids.

Mrs. Vanek: How do they do that?

Marta: Oh, they say things, and call them names, like *sissy*, or… or *fatso*, or things like that. They're bullies, that's what they are! Mean, nasty bullies!

Mr. Vanek: Do they pick on you?

Marta: No, but…the little kids… I think it hurts their feelings. And I think they're scared. And other kids kind of enjoy watching, like they think it's cool to pick on little kids.

Mrs. Vanek: Have you told Mr. Claude, your bus driver?

Marta: I don't want to be a tattletale. But it isn't right!

Mrs. Vanek: Well, I'll give Mr. Claude a call. And I'll try not to make things worse. They may not be bad boys, but what they're doing is bad and it should stop. Thank you for telling us. Now give me a hug.

9a (continuation)

Marta, Mrs. Vanek, Mr. Vanek
The following afternoon. Vanek living room

(Marta enters, slamming door)

Marta: *(shouting, angry)* I *don't* believe it!

Mrs. Vanek: What's the matter, dear?

Marta: Mr. Claude!

Mrs. Vanek: Your bus driver? What did he do?

Marta: You know those bullies I told you about?

Mrs. Vanek: Yes. I talked to Mr. Claude about them.

Chapter Two: SCHOOL

Marta: Well, he's... He's made them his *helpers*. They're supposed to make us all behave, but *they're* the worst! How could he do that?

Mr. Vanek: You mean, the bullies behave badly, so he gives them a kind of reward?

Marta: Yes. Isn't that stupid? Now when we get on the bus, *they're* the ones who get to make sure nobody cuts in line or pushes anyone else. And if kids are too noisy, *they* tell them to be quiet.

Mrs. Vanek: Oh that's not right. I'm going to call the principal this time. That shouldn't be.

Mr. Vanek: Wait a minute, Rose. Marta, did the bullies pick on those little kids today?

Marta: How could they? They were too busy bossing everyone around! It's like, they're mean and nasty, so now they're in charge.

Mr. Vanek: Maybe there's something we don't know. I think we should wait a week and see how things go. And then decide whether to call the principal again or not. What do you think, Rose?

Mrs. Vanek: Hmmm... When I talked to Mr. Claude, he said he had an idea but he didn't tell me what it was.

Mr. Vanek: Maybe that's his idea. Keep the bullies in line by giving them responsibility.

Mrs. Vanek: I hadn't thought of that. All right, let's wait and see what happens. Is that OK with you Marta?

Marta: Well... OK. But I still want to scream!

Mrs. Vanek: Not too loud. You'll break your father's glasses.

Mr. Vanek: Did I just see her smile?

Mrs. Vanek: No, she's just getting ready to scream.

Marta: Hey! Stop picking on me! Anyway, thanks. I love you two.

EXPANSION

Have you seen some students who pick on others? What has happened? Did it stop or continue? Talk about what you have seen.

10 Making Hypotheses

Sunita and Ron
Walking home from school

Sunita: Hipothe. Hippo. Hippy. Darn!
Ron: Hippopotamus? What are you talking about?
Sunita: I learned a new word today.
Ron: Really! What?
Sunita: Hippo. Hypo. Darn. It was so long!
Ron: Well, what does it mean?
Sunita: It's like a guess.
Ron: Why don't you just say "guess" then?
Sunita: Because I like to learn new words.
Ron: I hate to say it, but it doesn't sound like you've learned it yet.

10a (continuation)

Sunita and Mr. Chang
In school, the next day

Sunita: Mr. Chang, what was that big word from yesterday?
Mr. Chang: Which big word, Sunita?
Sunita: The big one that sounded like an elephant.
Mr. Chang: An elephant?
Sunita: You know, hippo something.
Mr. Chang: Hypothesis?
Sunita: Yes, that's it! Thanks!
Mr. Chang: Not so fast. Do you remember what it means?
Sunita: Oh, sure. It's like a guess.
Mr. Chang: Good for you. But it's a special kind of guess.
Sunita: I know that. It's a guess we use when we want to find out something.
Mr. Chang: You're right. Now you can get ready for your project.
Sunita: I know I can. I need to write a hypothe… Hypo…hippo… Hypopitus.
Mr. Chang: Hypothesis.
Sunita: Right. Hypothesis. Hypothesis. Hypothesis. Bye!

10b (continuation)
Frank, John, Rosemary, Sunita, Carlos, and Mr. Chang
In class, the next day

Mr. Chang: OK, class, does everyone have at least one hypothesis for a survey?

(Many students mumble affirmative responses.)

Mr. Chang: Good. Let's hear some of them. Frank?

Frank: There are more old textbooks in our class than new ones.

Mr. Chang: OK, that's something we can count. John?

John: Students eat more hamburgers at lunch than salads.

Mr. Chang: Good. Countable again. Rosemary?

Rosemary: There are more brown-eyed boys in this class than blue-eyed boys.

Mr. Chang: Well, that's certainly something you can observe. Sunita?

Sunita: There are more bad boys in our school than bad girls.

Mr. Chang: Hmmm…How would you know?

Sunita: I will find out how many boys get sent to the principal's office every day. And then how many girls.

Mr. Chang: Well, I guess that's one way to tell. Carlos?

Carlos: I'm sorry, Mr. Chang. I forgot to do my homework.

Mr. Chang: Well, then, why don't you stay after class today and we'll think of some hypotheses together.

Carlos: Great! Thanks!

EXPANSION

Write five countable hypotheses of your own.

11 Why Do We Call Him "Mr. Claude"?

Silvia and Rita
At school, in the cafeteria

Silvia: Rita, did you ever wonder why…

Rita: Why what, Silvia?

Silvia: Well, think about this. The principal's first name is Bill. But we call him Mr. Snyder. Our English teacher's first name is Carol. But we call her Mrs. Williams.

Rita: Yeah, so?

Silvia: Well, you know our bus driver's name is Claude Latour. Why do we call him Mr. Claude? Why don't we call him Mr. Latour?

Rita: Uh… I never thought about that.

Silvia: OK. Let's think. You use the first name with your friends. Or with any kids. But you use "Mr." and "Mrs.," "Miss," and "Ms." with grown-ups.

Rita: But you don't use "Mr." and then a first name.

Silvia: Let's go ask Mrs. Williams.

Rita: You mean "Mrs. Carol"?

Silvia: Eeew… That sounds so wrong!

11a (continuation)

Silvia, Rita, and Mrs. Williams
Later, in English class, after the lesson is over

Silvia: Mrs. Williams, could we ask you a question?

Mrs. Williams: Sure, girls. What is it?

Rita: It's about what we call people. Why do we call you "Mrs. Williams" and the principal "Mr. Snyder," but we call our bus driver "Mr. Claude"?

Mrs. Williams: That's a very good question! And I've thought about it a lot. Would you like a true answer?

Rita: Yes.

Mrs. Williams: The answer is… I don't know!

Both girls: You don't know?

Mrs. Williams: Well, I do and I don't.

Silvia: I don't understand.

Chapter Two: SCHOOL

Mrs. Williams:	Language is tricky. It mostly plays by rules, but not always. "Mr." and "Mrs." and "Ms." are polite and show respect.
Rita:	Yeah…
Mrs. Williams:	And first names are right for friends.
Rita:	Yeah. So we call Mr. Claude "Mr. Claude" because we respect him *and* he's our friend.
Silvia:	But Mrs. Williams is our friend too! And so is Mr. Snyder. But I'm not going to call him "Bill" or even "Mr. Bill."
Mrs. Williams:	Right. Can I think about this some more, and we can talk tomorrow?
Rita and Silvia:	Sure.

11b (continuation)
The next day

Rita:	So, Mrs. Williams, did you think about it?
Mrs. Williams:	Yes, a lot. And I asked some other teachers, too.
Silvia:	And?
Mrs. Williams:	So here's what I think. There is a long tradition with teachers and principals—going back to even before there were buses. They represent schools and education. Parents and everyone want to be sure that young people respect their teachers and principals, because learning is so important.
Rita:	But bus driving is important too. We wouldn't even *get* to school if it weren't for Mr. Claude. And we respect him!
Mrs. Williams:	Right. You see why I don't know the answer? And there's more. Look at other bus drivers in the school. Mr. Fredericks is "Mr. Fredericks," not "Mr. Mike." And Jimmy—Mr. Petro—is "Jimmy," not "Mr. Jimmy" or "Mr. Petro."
Silvia:	Stop! My head is spinning! How do we know which to use?
Mrs. Williams:	I think it's what the students and the bus driver are all comfortable with. Why don't you ask Mr. Claude what he thinks?
Rita:	Maybe we'll try that.

11c (continuation)
Silvia, Rita, and Mr. Claude
Later that afternoon, on the school bus

Silvia:	Mr. Claude, why do we call you "Mr. Claude"?
Mr. Claude	Because that's my name! What do you think you should call me, Abraham Lincoln?
Rita:	*(laughing)* No, but you're the only person we know where we say "Mr." and your first name.
Silvia:	Do you like being called "Mr. Claude"?
Mr. Claude	Well…yes!
Silvia:	What if we called you "Mr. Latour"?
Mr. Claude	Oh, no. I wouldn't like that. It would make me feel…too far away from you. Too high up.
Rita:	What about just "Claude"?
Mr. Claude	I don't like that either. I'm a little different from all your other friends, but not too different! A little respect is good. But not too much!
Silvia:	OK.
Mr. Claude	It's sort of like you say "Uncle Frank" or "Aunt Teresa." Those are people who are close to you, but you still show proper respect.
Silvia:	Oh, that's a good explanation!
Rita:	Yeah, that makes sense.
Mr. Claude	And I like "Mr. Claude." That's who I am. That's who I've always been in school. And that's who I want to be! Now here we are at your house. Get off the bus. You're making me think too hard!
Both girls:	OK. Thanks! Bye, Mr. Claude!

EXPANSION

Make a list of all the people that you call Mr., Mrs., or Ms. Do you call any of them by their first names? Why?

12 Cast Your Vote!

Juan and Jay
In the hallway on Election Day

Juan: Hurry up, we're late for class!

Jay: I'm hurrying, but there are so many people in the halls today.

Juan: Yeah. It feels strange to see so many grown-ups at school.

Jay: That's because our school is a real polling place for the presidential election. The grown-ups are going to the cafeteria to vote.

Juan: And we get to vote, too!

Jay: Right. In the music room. But our votes don't count.

Juan: Do you know who you'll vote for?

Jay: I think so. We had so many discussions in class, but now I can't really remember the details. How about you?

Juan: I'm going to keep it simple and vote for the same person my parents are voting for.

Jay: Who's that?

Juan: I can't tell you! It's a secret ballot, remember?

12a (continuation)

Mrs. Hirsch, Juan, Jay, and Salma
In the classroom

Mrs. Hirsch: Class, in a few minutes we'll go to the music room to vote. We'll use real voting machines, too, just like the grown-ups are using today.

Juan: Mrs. Hirsch, are the voting machines hard to understand?

Mrs. Hirsch: Not really. They're a lot like the computers you use in the writing lab. You just click your mouse on the name of the person you want for president. I will be there if you need help.

Jay: Oh, good.

Mrs. Hirsch: Any other questions?

Juan: What happened to the pictures of the candidates?

Salma: And the posters we made about their promises?

Mrs. Hirsch: We had to remove all election materials by law.

Jay:	By law? Why?
Mrs. Hirsch:	Because every election needs to be as fair as possible. There can't be pictures or posters within 100 feet of the polling place. And people can't tell you who to vote for near the polling place, either.
Juan:	But we're not really voting.
Mrs. Hirsch:	Yes, that's right. But the adults you've seen around the building are.
Juan:	Oh, yeah! That makes sense.
Mrs. Hirsch:	Now let's go to the music room to vote.

12b (continuation)
Mrs. Hirsch, Jay, Juan, and Salma
In the classroom during the week following the presidential election

Mrs. Hirsch:	Today, class, we get to vote again.
Jay:	Are we going to elect another president already?
Mrs. Hirsch:	No, we're going to decide which movie the whole school will see when the December exams are finished.
Juan:	Where will they show it?
Mrs. Hirsch:	In the same place as last year, the auditorium.
Salma:	Do we get to use real machines again?
Mrs. Hirsch:	No, they went back to the County Board of Elections. This time, we'll use paper ballots. But they're still secret.
Jay:	What are the choices?
Mrs. Hirsch:	You have three choices. They're listed on the ballots I'm about to give you.
Juan:	But wait a minute! What if we don't know anything about the three movies?
Mrs. Hirsch:	Hmmmm… Good point.

Salma: Tell us what the movies are, and then we can tell you if we know about them all.

Mrs. Hirsch: Wait a minute. I have an idea. I'll tell you the name of each movie. Then we'll find four people who know about it. At lunchtime, they can work here in the classroom and make a poster.

Mrs. Hirsch: And then, when you come back after lunch, we'll take some time to look at each of the three posters.

Jay: And then we have to take the posters down before we vote.

Mrs. Hirsch: Right!

EXPANSION

Do students in your school vote in real or imaginary elections? Do they vote for people (like a president or student leader) or for plans (like what movies to see or what to have in the school lunchroom)? Make a list of five more things that students could vote for in your school.

THE WIDER WORLD

1 Riding a Bike

Lucy (an eight year-old) and Mr. Humphrey (a neighbor)
In Lucy's driveway

Mr. Humphrey:	Hi Lucy. What have you got there?
Lucy:	Oh hi, Mr. Humphrey. I've got a new bike.
Mr. Humphrey:	Oh it's beautiful! A two-wheeler.
Lucy:	There's only one problem.
Mr. Humphrey:	What's that?
Lucy:	I don't know how to ride it. I never had a bike before.
Mr. Humphrey:	Well, here. Try riding it while I hold it up.
Lucy:	Are you sure I won't fall?
Mr. Humphrey:	Everyone falls sometime. But you'll be OK.
Lucy:	What should I do?
Mr. Humphrey:	Just start moving forward.
Lucy:	Yiii… I'm going to fall!
Mr. Humphrey:	No you're not. I've got you. You're doing fine.
Lucy:	Don't let go!
Mr. Humphrey:	Actually, I did for a few seconds there. You were riding it on your own.
Lucy:	I was?
Mr. Humphrey:	Yup. Once a bike starts moving, it stays up and doesn't fall over.
Lucy:	Always?
Mr. Humphrey:	Well, no. Sometimes it falls. But it didn't fall just now.
Lucy:	Wow! I rode my bike!
Mr. Humphrey:	So, you can do it now, right?
Lucy:	Yes, I can. But will you come over again tomorrow?

EXPANSION

Tell a friend about a neighbor who helped you.

Chapter Three: THE WIDER WORLD

2 Stranger Danger

Samantha and Mrs. Thomas
In the school hallway

Samantha: Mrs. Thomas! Mrs. Thomas.

Mrs. Thomas: What is it Samantha? You're all out of breath! And you're crying!

Samantha: I was just walking to school, and…and…

Mrs. Thomas: It's OK, dear. You're here now, and you're safe. What is it? What happened?

Samantha: I… I… (cries)

Mrs. Thomas: It's all right. Here. Hold my hands. Look at me. Take a deep breath. Good girl. Now, what happened?

Samantha: I was… I was walking to school, and a man brought his car alongside of me.

Mrs. Thomas: Oh, dear.

Samantha: He said he'd give me a ride. I said no.

Mrs. Thomas: Good for you.

Samantha: Then he said he had a puppy to show me. I said no again, and kept walking.

Mrs. Thomas: That was the right thing to do.

Samantha: But he kept driving alongside of me and looking at me. So I ran the rest of the way to school.

Mrs. Thomas: You did exactly the right thing. Come with me to the office now. It's all right. Hold my hand. We're going to call the police. Do you remember what color the car was?

Samantha: It was yellow. But it was old. It had rust spots all over it.

Mrs. Thomas: Excellent. You're going to be fine. You're a brave and very smart girl. You stay right with me today. We'll call your mom and dad too, OK?

Samantha: Thank you, Mrs. Thomas.

EXPANSION

If a stranger ever tries to get you or your friends into a car, tell a teacher and your parents right away.

3 Let *Us* Do the Shopping!

Chris, Phil (brothers), and Mrs. Vitakis
At the Vitakis house

Chris: Can we all—the whole family—go to a movie tonight?
Mrs. Vitakis: Well, I don't think so.
Chris: Why not?
Mrs. Vitakis: I haven't been to the store all week. There's nothing in the house.
Chris: Nothing? Look at all this stuff in the kitchen.
Mrs. Vitakis: Well, OK. There are some things in the house. But nothing that I need to make tomorrow's dinner for your grandparents, your aunt, and your uncle.
Chris: What if we go shopping for you tomorrow morning?
Mrs. Vitakis: We?
Chris: Phil and me.
Phil: Yeah, Chris and I could do it.
Mrs. Vitakis: You could?
Chris: Sure, just make us a list.
Mrs. Vitakis: Well…
Chris: Don't you think we can read?
Mrs. Vitakis: Well…
Phil: Give us a chance!
Mrs. Vitakis: Well…
Chris: Aw, come on, Mom.
Mrs. Vitakis: Well… OK. I've been wanting to go to a movie anyway.
Phil: Great! We'll all go to a movie tonight, and Chris and I will shop tomorrow morning.
Mrs. Vitakis: Good. And I'll clean up the house while you're shopping.

3a (continuation)
The next day

Mrs. Vitakis: Good morning, boys. Time to get up!
Chris & Phil: Get up??? We just went to bed.
Mrs. Vitakis: Sure, eight hours ago.
Chris: So what's the hurry? It's Saturday.
Mrs. Vitakis: Right. It's Saturday...all day. Do you remember anything special about Saturday?
Chris: Ooooohhh...shopping.
Mrs. Vitakis: You bet. On your feet!
Chris: OK. OK. That was a great movie last night. I just forgot about shopping for a minute. Phil? Rise and shine.
Phil: I'll do my best.

3b (continuation)
Chris and Phil
At the grocery store

Phil: You know, Chris, shopping isn't so bad.
Chris: I agree. I don't know why our sisters complain so much about it.
Phil: Let's see... What's next on the list? Milk.
Chris: Over here.
Phil: What kind do we get?
Chris: I have no idea. Let's just get something.
Phil: This says "two percent." What does that mean?
Chris: Who knows? It has a purple label. I like purple. Let's get that.
Phil: Fine. Next...eggs.
Chris: But look at all the eggs? Small, medium, large, extra large, jumbo! And then over here, Omega-3 eggs. What's that?
Phil: Let's get big eggs.
Chris: That's jumbo.
Phil: Good. Meat is next. Chicken.

Chris: That's easy. I know about chicken.
Phil: Sure, you do. Look at the choices!
Chris: Skinless, boneless, thighs, tenders, half chickens, uh-oh.
Phil: Chris, I think we have a problem here.
Chris: You're right. I had no idea that we needed to make so many choices.
Phil: What will we do?
Chris: Let's give up. Put everything back.
Phil: Yes, and go home. Talk to our sisters.
Chris: I know they will go shopping for us, but what will they make us do in return?

EXPANSION

Make a grocery shopping list. Beside each item, write the decision or decisions you will make about it; for example, eggs—medium.

4 Going to the Mall

 *Marcia and Eliza*
On the telephone

Marcia: Hello?
Eliza: Hi, Marcia. It's me, Eliza.
Marcia: Oh, hi, Eliza. What are you doing?
Eliza: Not much. I'm bored. Let's go to the mall!
Marcia: Sure. But my mom says I can't go alone.
Eliza: Well, you're not going alone. You're going with me.
Marcia: I mean, I can't go with just kids.
Eliza: Hmmm… I could ask my big sister to take us. She's eighteen.
Marcia: That'll work.
Eliza: And besides, she can drive us there.
Marcia: Even better! What time should I be ready?
Eliza: Around eleven o'clock, I think. I'll call you if there's any problem.
Marcia: Thanks, Eliza! I'll see you then.

4a (continuation)
Marcia, Eliza, and Lana (Eliza's big sister)
At the mall

Marcia: Lana, thanks so much for taking us to the mall.
Lana: No problem. I need to look for a pair of jeans anyway.
Eliza: Good! We'll help you look.
Lana: What do you two need?
Eliza: Oh, nothing. We were just bored and looking for something to do.
Marcia: Yeah. And even if we don't buy anything, we can look at stuff.
Eliza: And wish we were rich so we could buy it all!
Marcia: Mostly we just wanted to hang out.
Lana: I know what that means, look for cute boys.
Eliza: Who, us?
Lana: Look, here's a place where I can get some nice jeans. Let's go in.
Marcia: I see where the jeans are—over here.
Lana: Nice selection… Oh, I love this pair!

Eliza: They're not too expensive, are they?
Lana: No, but will they be too tight?
Marcia: I don't think so. I think they'll look good on you.
Eliza: But maybe you should try them on to be sure.
Lana: OK, I'll try them on. If they fit, I'll buy them. Then you two can go out and look for some more cute boys!

EXPANSION

Write a dialogue that shows you and some of your friends shopping or hanging out at the mall. What kinds of things do you talk about?

Chapter Three: THE WIDER WORLD

5 What Size Are You?

Boris and Mr. Katz (salesperson)
At the clothing store

Mr. Katz: Hello, young man. Can I help you?
Boris: Yes, please. I need pants for school.
Mr. Katz: Sure. What size?
Boris: I... I... I don't know American sizes.
Mr. Katz: I see. Well, you look like a size 14.
Boris: OK.
Mr. Katz: What color do you like?
Boris: I don't know. Maybe blue.
Mr. Katz: Ah, yes. Navy.
Boris: Yes, navy blue.
Mr. Katz: Here are some navy blue fourteens.
Boris: OK. Thanks.
Mr. Katz: And why don't you try these dark green ones?
Boris: OK.
Mr. Katz: The changing room is over there.
Boris: Over where?
Mr. Katz: Right over there. I'll show you.

5a (variation)
At the clothing store

Mr. Katz: Hello, young man. Can I help you?
Boris: Yes, please. I need a warm winter coat.
Mr. Katz: Sure. What size?
Boris: I...I...I don't know American sizes.
Mr. Katz: I see. Well, you look like a medium.
Boris: OK.
Mr. Katz: What color do you like?
Boris: I don't know. Maybe this color.
Mr. Katz: Ah, yes. Charcoal gray.
Boris: Yes, gray.

Mr. Katz:	Here is a nice gray medium.
Boris:	OK. Thanks.
Mr. Katz:	And why don't you try this plaid?
Boris:	OK.
Mr. Katz:	You can try them on right here. There's a mirror over there.
Boris:	Thanks.

EXPANSION

Make a list of your clothes. Name each item, its size, and its color. Are there any that are too small?

Chapter Three: THE WIDER WORLD

6 At the Grocer's

Katina and Mr. Oshinski

At the grocery store

Mr. Oshinski: Well hello there, young lady.
Katina: Hello, Mr. Oshinski.
Mr. Oshinski: How may I help you today?
Katina: My mother sent me to get some hamburger.
Mr. Oshinski: Well, you came to the right place! How much do you want?
Katina: Um, I don't know. I forgot to ask my mom how much to get.
Mr. Oshinski: Well, we could give her a call. Do you know your phone number?
Katina: Oh, yes.
Mr. Oshinski: Here then. Use my phone.

6a (continuation)

Katina and Mrs. Peters

(Phone rings.)
Mrs. Peters: Hello?
Katina: Hi, Mom. It's me.
Mrs. Peters: Oh. Why are you calling? Is everything all right?
Katina: Oh yes, everything's fine. But I forgot to ask how much hamburger I should buy. Mr. Oshinski let me use his phone.
Mrs. Peters: That's very kind of him. We need a pound and a half of hamburger.
Katina: OK, Mom.
Mrs. Peters: And be sure to say thank you to Mr. Oshinski.
Katina: I will, Mom. Bye.

EXPANSION

When you go to the store, do you ever discover that you don't have enough information to buy what you need? Say the dialogue again with something different than hamburger.
If you can't think of anything, try the dialogue with sugar. You don't know if your mother wanted a one-pound box or a five-pound bag.

7 Open Wide!

Ruth Cholok (a 12-year old girl) and Dr. Frommer (the dentist)

Dr. Frommer's office

Dr. Frommer:	Hi, Ruth. Well, let's get started. Open wide. That's it. Good girl.
	(pause)
Dr. Frommer:	So, what did you do in school today?
Ruth:	Ah-waa. Ehhh. Ah ant ohk.
Dr. Frommer:	Oh, sorry! I guess you can't talk when I've got my fingers in your mouth. There, is that better?
Ruth:	Yes. We learned a lot of new English words. And we learned a song. "If you're happy and you know it, then your face will surely show it, if you're—"
Dr. Frommer:	OK, you don't have to sing the whole thing. I've got work to do. Open.
Ruth:	Ahhh…
Dr. Frommer:	If your face is going to show you're happy, then you need to smile. If you need to smile, you need nice teeth. That's what I'm here for.
Ruth:	Uhhh…
Dr. Frommer:	I'm going to fix a cavity, but first I'll give you a shot so that it won't hurt.
Ruth:	O-ay.
Dr. Frommer:	Here it comes. Little pinprick.
Ruth:	Owww!
Dr. Frommer:	There. All done. Now you won't feel the drill or anything.
Ruth:	The… The drill?
Dr. Frommer:	It won't hurt. I promise.
Ruth:	OK. I believe you… I think.
Dr. Frommer:	You'll be fine. And you'll have a beautiful smile to go with that happy face.
	(a short time later)
Dr. Frommer:	OK. All done. I'll just rinse your mouth. *(pause).* There. Now spit!

Chapter Three: THE WIDER WORLD

7a (continuation)
Ruth, Mr. Cholok, Mrs. Cholok
At home

Mr. Cholok:	Hello, Ruth. How was your visit to the dentist?
Ruth:	I think Dr. Frommer is crazy, Dad.
Mrs. Cholok:	Why is that?
Ruth:	Well, first he sticks his fingers in my mouth. Then he asks me questions.
Mr. Cholok:	Maybe he was just making a joke.
Ruth:	No, I think he's crazy.
Mrs. Cholok:	Well, did he fix your teeth?
Ruth:	Yes. I had one cavity. But I hate that drill! Grrrrr.
Mrs. Cholok:	Did it hurt?
Ruth:	Well, no. Not after he gave me a shot. But the needle hurt!
Mr. Cholok:	Oh, my poor, poor baby.
Ruth:	Dad! You're making fun of me!
Mr. Cholok:	Heh-heh. You're right, dear. I guess I am.
Mrs. Cholok:	But, Dr. Frommer... He can't be all bad if he fixed your teeth.
Ruth:	I guess you're right. I guess he's a nice man. But I hope I never have to see him again!
Mr. Cholok:	Um. Should I tell her, or should you?
Ruth:	Tell me what?
Mrs. Cholok:	Well dear... You've got an appointment for a check-up in six months.

EXPANSION

Have you been to the dentist in North America? Have your friends? Talk with them about what it was like.

8 Gone Fishing

Rashid and Will
Saturday, in their bedroom

Rashid: Will! Wake up!
Will: Ehhh... Blaaa... Don't want to. I'm sleepy.
Rashid: It's Saturday!
Will: Good. No school. Sleep some more. Go away.
Rashid: We're going fishing!
Will: *(Wide awake, jumping out of bed.)* Oh! I forgot! Let's go!
Rashid: Put your clothes on first.
Will: Oh, yeah.
(pause)
Rashid: Have you got everything?
Will: Yup.
Rashid: Fishing rod?
Will: Oh, forgot. Where is it?
Rashid: In the basement. Go get it.
Will: OK. *(He leaves. Sound of footsteps leaving.)*
(Pause. Sound of footsteps returning.)
Will: Rod. Got it.
Rashid: Reel?
Will: Oops. Forgot that too. What else?
Rashid: Worms.
Will: I don't have any worms!
Rashid: That's OK. We'll dig some when we get there.
Will: OK. I'll go get my reel.

8a (continuation)
On the bus

Will: Does this bus go all the way to the bay?
Rashid: Yes. I've done it before.
Will: What kind of fish do you catch in the bay?
Rashid: Oh, maybe sunfish. Or carp. Bass, if we're lucky.
Will: I think I'll be lucky.
Rashid: Here we are! OK. Get off the bus.
Will: OK. *(looking around)* Rashid! I don't see any place to dig worms.

Rashid: Me neither. But there's a bait shop over there.
Will: Do you have any money?
Rashid: Didn't you bring money?
Will: Oh yeah. I forgot. I have two dollars.
Rashid: That should be enough for worms. Go get some, little brother.

8b (continuation)
On the banks of the bay

Rashid: OK. Cast it out there.
Will: Where?
Rashid: Out *there*. Anywhere that you see water.
Will: Where are *you* going to cast?
Rashid: Somewhere else.
Will: I want to cast where you cast. You know where the fish are.
Rashid: Will! If you do that, our lines will get all tied up with each other!
Will: You worry too much, my brother.

8c (continuation)
An hour later

Rashid: Have you had any nibbles yet?
Will: No! Have you?
Rashid: No!
(pause)
Rashid: Will! I've got one. I've got one!
Will: One what?
Rashid: A fish!
Will: Oh. Good! Reel him in!
Rashid: He's coming in! He's coming in! He's fighting hard! Oh heck. He got away.
Will: Too bad, my friend.
(pause)
Will: Whoa! What's this?
Rashid: What's what?
Will: Something's pulling on my line.
Rashid: It's a fish, Will. Reel it in!
Will: Oh! OK. Here we go!

Rashid: Good! You're getting it, you're getting it. Bring him in. OK! I've got him in the net.
Will: Big, isn't he?
Rashid: Well, about three and a half inches.

8d (continuation)

Rashid, Will, Mr. Gannon, and Mrs. Gannon.

That night, at the dinner table

Mr. Gannon: So, boys, you went fishing today. What did you catch?
Rashid: Will caught one.
Mr. Gannon: Good for you, Will! Was he big?
Will: Oh, yes. Very big.
Mrs. Gannon: How big?
Will: Very big. Very big.
Rashid: Not so big.
Mrs. Gannon: Did he put up a good fight?
Will: Oh yes. Very good fight!
Rashid: It took about 10 seconds to reel him in.
Mrs. Gannon: Rashid. You sound jealous. Did you catch anything today?
Rashid: Oh yes. I caught a big one. Bigger than Will's. And he fought harder too.
Mrs. Gannon: So you boys caught these great big fish. Why didn't you bring them home so I could cook them for dinner?
Rashid: Well, Will's was only about three and a half inches long.
Will: And Rashid's got away.

EXPANSION

Will says his fish was "Very big. Very big." It wasn't. It was tiny. Will was **exaggerating.** *Ask someone what* **exaggeration** *means, if you don't know. Then think of times when you or someone else exaggerated and describe what happened.*

Chapter Three: THE WIDER WORLD

9 What Are Friends For?

 *Jeannine, Maria, and a vendor*
At the park

Jeannine: It's so hot today!
Maria: I know! My throat is so dry. I wish I'd brought some water with us to the park.
Jeannine: Me too!
Maria: Look! There's a man selling cold drinks!
Jeannine: I don't have any money.
Maria: I do!
Jeannine: Then let's go! I'll race you there!
Vendor: Hello, girls. May I help you?
Maria: I'd like to buy a couple of soft drinks, please.
Vendor: Sure. What size and what kind?
Maria: I'd like lemon-lime.
Jeannine: And I'd like a root beer.
Maria: Large! We both want large.
Vendor: All right. That will be three dollars and fifty cents.
Maria: Two fifty, two seventy-five, two eighty-five... oh no! I only have two dollars and eighty-five cents!
Vendor: You could buy two small ones. They're only one dollar and forty cents each.
Maria: OK, thanks! Here's two dollars and eighty cents.
Jeannine: Thanks, Maria! This will save my life!
Maria: What are friends for?

9a (continuation)
A short time later

Jeannine: Wow! This is the best root beer I've ever tasted!
Maria: I agree! I am so thirsty! Oh no! *(sound of a bottle dropping)*
Jeannine: You dropped it!
Maria: Oh, it's spilled all over!
Jeannine: Come on. Let's go back and ask the man if he has a cup. Then you can share mine.
Maria: Oh thank you Jeannine! That's really nice of you.
Jeannine: No problem. What are friends for?

9b (continuation)
Back at the vendor's

Jeannine: Hello, sir!

Vendor: Well, hello, girls. What brings you back?

Maria: We had a little accident.

Vendor: Uh-oh. What happened?

Maria: Well, as I started to drink my lemon-lime, the bottle slipped out of my hand…

Jeannine: And it smashed on the sidewalk…

Maria: I'm so clumsy!

Vendor: That's too bad! On a hot day like this!

Jeannine: But it's OK. She can share my root beer. Would you have a paper cup we could use?

Vendor: I think I could give you one. But I have a better idea.

Maria: What's that?

Vendor: Well, as I recall, you still have a nickel, don't you?

Maria: Yes. But that's all.

Vendor: And you're both good friends, right?

Jeannine: Oh, yes!

Vendor: Well, I have a really, really cold bottle of lemon-lime right here.

Maria: But we don't have enough money!

Vendor: Hold on. It just so happens that two minutes ago, I started to have a friendship sale.

Jeannine: What's a friendship sale?

Vendor: During a friendship sale, this really, really cold bottle of lemon-lime costs exactly… Let me see here now… I have to figure this out on my calculator… Ah yes! *Five cents*!

EXPANSION

Think of a time when a friend did something nice for you. Describe it to your teacher or to other friends.

Chapter Three: THE WIDER WORLD

10 A Visit to the Zoo

Miguel and Gabriela
Class field trip to the zoo

Miguel: Hi, Gabriela.
Gabriela: Hi, Miguel.
Miguel: Have you been to the zoo before?
Gabriela: No, have you?
Miguel: Oh, yes. Lots of times. Stay with me. I'll show you neat stuff.
Gabriela: OK.
Miguel: Like right here. Snakes and turtles and stuff. What does that sign say?
Gabriela: Reptiles.
Miguel: Oh good. You read English better than I do. Look at that snake! What is it?
Gabriela: *(reading)* Um. It says, um, "Bur-mese Py-thon."
Miguel: Eiieew. How would you like to find one of those under your bed?
Gabriela: Shut up, Miguel. Let's go someplace else.
Miguel: OK. Over here.

10a (continuation)
A few minutes later

Miguel: You'll like these. Elephants!
Gabriela: Wow! They're so big!
Miguel: Come on. Let's get closer.
Gabriela: Just a little. Look, he's sticking his—what do you call that?
Miguel: His *trunk*.
Gabriela: He's sticking his trunk in the water. Now he's picking it up and pointing it at... At you, Miguel! Oh! Look out!!
Miguel: Ahhhhhh!
Gabriela: Miguel! You're soaked!
Miguel: Don't worry. I'm fine. Let's go somewhere else.
Gabriela: You look pretty silly, Miguel. All wet like that.
Miguel: Don't let the other kids see me, OK?
Gabriela: You look pretty silly. Like you fell in a lake or something.
Miguel: Oh, be quiet. Look. Come over here.

10b (continuation)
A few minutes later

Miguel: Look at those.

Gabriela: What are they?

Miguel: I don't know, but they're cool. Read the label to me.

Gabriela: Baboons.

Miguel: Yeah, baboons. Watch. They climb all over everything. And they carry their babies underneath them. There's one!

Gabriela: Oh yeah! Oh that's so cute! The little baby is just holding on!

Miguel: Yup. Come on, Gabriela. I want to show you the polar bears.

Gabriela: Oh. Where are they from?

Miguel: Way up north.

Gabriela: That's a big help. Where I come from—Argentina—everything is *way up north*.

10c (continuation)
A few minutes later

Miguel: OK. There he is. The polar bear.

Gabriela: Wow! He's so white.

Miguel: Do you know why?

Gabriela: No, why?

Miguel: Because where he lives—up north—not just north of Argentina, but *really* north, like at the North Pole—there's a lot of snow. He's white so that he looks like the snow, and bigger animals can't see him and eat him.

Gabriela: What animals are bigger than he is?

Miguel: Uh… Now that you mention it… Uh… I don't think there are any. I wonder why he *is* so white.

Gabriela: You know, we better find the teacher and the other kids pretty soon.

Miguel: Maybe not quite yet, Gabriela. My clothes are still pretty wet. Look! Over there! I think it's… Yes! Penguins! Come on! I'll show you!

EXPANSION

How many different animals can you name in English? Make a list. Compare your list with a friend's list.

10d (continuation)
A few minutes later

Miguel: See? There they are. The penguins.

Gabriela: Oh, look how black and white they are!

Miguel: Like they were wearing... Oh, what's that word?

Gabriela: What word?

Miguel: You know. What men wear when they get all dressed up and fancy.

Gabriela: Oh, I know. *Tuxedo*.

Miguel: Tuxedo?

Gabriela: Yes. They get all dressed up in a white shirt, and a black coat, and a bow tie.

Miguel: Tuxedo. Okay, I'll remember that.

Gabriela: Where do penguins come from?

Miguel: Way down south—further south than Argentina. Near the South Pole, where there is a lot of snow and ice, like at the North Pole.

Gabriela: Miguel, you're shivering. You must be really cold!

Miguel: Well look where we've been!

Gabriela: Huh?

Miguel: We've been to the North Pole with polar bears, and to the South Pole with penguins! And besides...my clothes are still wet!

CHAPTER 4
JUST FOR FUN

1 Stories of Nasruddin

Omar: Nasruddin, what was that big noise I heard coming from your house yesterday?

Nasruddin: Oh, my wife threw a bundle of dirty laundry down the stairs.

Omar: A bundle of laundry? But laundry is soft. I heard a big thump! Laundry shouldn't make that much noise.

Nasruddin: There was a lot of laundry.

Omar: That still doesn't explain it! I heard a great big noise.

Nasruddin: Well, I have one shirt that is very big.

Omar: But, Nasruddin, how could any shirt, even a big one, make that much noise?

Nasruddin: Maybe because I was wearing it at the time.

1a (continuation)

Omar: Nasruddin, why are you crawling around on your hands and knees?

Nasruddin: I lost my ring, and I can't find it anywhere.

Omar: Oh, that's too bad. Can I help you?

Nasruddin: Sure, maybe if we both crawl around, we'll be able to find it.

Omar: OK. Do you remember exactly where you were when you lost it?

Nasruddin: Of course I do. I was down in the basement.

Omar: Down in the basement! But then, why are we crawling around up here in the living room?

Nasruddin: Don't be silly, Omar. It's dark in the basement. How do you think we could find anything in the dark?

1b (continuation)

Omar: Nasruddin, come down from your roof. I have to ask you a question.
Nasruddin: Hello, Omar. Can't you ask it while I'm still on the roof?
Omar: No. It's very important. Climb down the ladder.
Nasruddin: All right, here I come. Now what's this very important question?
Omar: Could I borrow some money from you?
Nasruddin: Let me think about it. Follow me up on the roof.
Omar: Why do we have to go way up there?
Nasruddin: Just climb up the ladder. Then I will answer your question.
Omar: OK, here I come. This is a very hard climb!
Nasruddin: You're almost there. Just a few more steps.
Omar: OK, here I am. Now, can I borrow some money? What's your answer?
Nasruddin: The answer is no.

1c (continuation)
The Donkey

Omar: Hello, Nasruddin.
Nasruddin: Well, hello, Omar. What's on your mind?
Omar: I was wondering if I could borrow your donkey.
Nasruddin: I'm sorry, Omar. I would love to loan you my donkey, but yesterday my brother came all the way from his village to borrow my donkey, so I loaned it to him. It's not here.
Omar: Well, thank you anyway, Nasruddin. You are very generous.
Nasruddin: Don't mention it, Omar.
(donkey noises)
Omar: Wait a minute! I just heard your donkey bray! I thought you said it wasn't here!
Nasruddin: For heaven's sakes, Omar. Who are you going to believe? Me? Or a stupid donkey?

EXPANSION

Decide which is your favorite Nasruddin story and tell it to a friend.

2 Knock-Knock Jokes

Johnny: Knock-knock.
Margarita: Who's there?
Johnny: Fortification.
Margarita: Fortification who?
Johnny: Fortification, we decided to go to Florida.
Margarita: Fortification? Huh? I don't get it.
Johnny: For...ti...fication. Get it?
Margarita: Well...
Johnny: *For...the...vacation.*
Margarita: Oh! I got it! For the vacation, you're going to Florida!

2a (variation)

Johnny: Knock-knock.
Margarita: Who's there?
Johnny: Mister Walter.
Margarita: Mister Walter who?
Johnny: You don't Mister Walter until the well runs dry.
Margarita: This one doesn't make sense. Help me!
Johnny: Think of *Mister* as *miss the*. And think of *Walter* as *water*.
Margarita: Ick. I get it, but it's a dumb joke. Try again.

2b (variation)

Johnny: Knock-knock.
Margarita: Who's there?
Johnny: Carl.
Margarita: Carl who?
Johnny: Carl get you there faster than a bike.
Margarita: Carl? I don't get it. Carl's a boy's name.
Johnny: *Carl* means car *will*.
Margarita: Oh, I got it! A car will get you there faster than a bike!

2c (variation)

Johnny: Knock-knock.
Margarita: Who's there?
Johnny: Justin.
Margarita: Justin who?

Chapter Four: JUST FOR FUN

Johnny: Justin time for supper!
Margarita: Oh good. I get this one. *Just in time* for supper!

2d (variation)

Johnny: Knock-knock.
Margarita: Who's there?
Johnny: Ida.
Margarita: Ida who?
Johnny: Ida called before I came over, but your phone isn't working.
Margarita: Oh, I thought I was getting good at these, but I don't get it. Help me out.
Johnny: *Ida* is *I would have*, but we say *I wouldda*, which sounds a lot like *Ida*.

2e (variation)

Johnny: Knock-knock.
Margarita: Who's there?
Johnny: Dewey.
Margarita: Dewey who?
Johnny: Dewey have to listen to these jokes all night?
Margarita: Ugh. I know I should understand these jokes by now…
Johnny: I'll give you a hint. *Dewey* means *Do we*.
Margarita: OK. I've almost got it. *Do we*…. Can you say the rest again?
Johnny: Sure. Dewey have to listen to these jokes all night?
Margarita: *(moans)* OK. I got it. Can we stop now?

EXPANSION

Try these jokes on your friends and family. Maybe after a while, you will not have so many friends!

3 Does He Bite?

Louis and Luz (brother and sister), Mr. Bagwell (neighbor)
In the neighborhood

Louis:	Hey, Luz, look! There's Mr. Bagwell walking a dog.
Luz:	Hi, Mr. Bagwell!
Mr. Bagwell:	Well, hello, my young friends.
Louis:	That's a nice dog.
Luz:	What's its name?
Mr. Bagwell:	His name is Elvis.
Louis:	What kind of dog is it?
Mr. Bagwell:	Well, I'd say it's a mixture of about 6 different kinds.
Luz:	Does your dog bite?
Mr. Bagwell:	No.
Louis:	Oh good. I'll pet it.
Mr. Bagwell:	Maybe that's not a good id—
Louis:	Ouch! He bit me!
Luz:	Mr. Bagwell! I thought you said your dog didn't bite!
Mr. Bagwell:	I did. But this isn't *my* dog. It's *my* neighbor's dog.
Louis:	What? I don't understand.
Mr. Bagwell:	My neighbor asked me to take him for a walk. My dog's a Dalmatian. And *he's* very friendly.

EXPANSION

Try telling this joke to a friend. Do you know other similar jokes? Try telling them too. Ask your friends if they know any jokes like this one.

4 I Can Read Your Mind

Kevin and George
At George's house

Kevin: I can read your mind.
George: What do you mean?
Kevin: I can tell you your birthday.
George: Really?
Kevin: Yep. Month, day, and year.
George: *(skeptical)* Oh, sure.
Kevin: Do you want to try?
George: Yep.
Kevin: OK. First, let's get a calculator.
George: I have one somewhere. Just a minute.
Kevin: I'll wait.
George: Here it is.
Kevin: Good. Now, we start with your birth month.
George: What's a birth month?
Kevin: It's a number. Like if you were born in January, it's 1.
George: I see. Like if you were born in March—I wasn't—it's 3.
Kevin: That's right. So write down your birth month.
George: Done.
Kevin: Add 18.
George: Yep.
Kevin: Multiply by 25.
George: Uh-huh.
Kevin: Subtract 333.
George: Now what?
Kevin: Multiply by 8.
George: I'm glad I have a calculator. Are we done yet?
Kevin: About halfway. Don't give up.

4a (continuation)

Kevin: Subtract 554.
George: OK.
Kevin: Divide by 2. Add your birth date.
George: Date?

Kevin:	The number. Like if you were born on January sixteenth, you write 16.
George:	I see.
Kevin:	And don't tell me.
George:	OK.
Kevin:	Now, multiply by 5.
George:	Uh-hum.
Kevin:	Add 692.
George:	How much?
Kevin:	692.
George:	Got it. Are we almost done?
Kevin:	Almost. Multiply by 20.
George:	OK.

4b (continuation)

Kevin:	Now, you know the year that you were born, right?
George:	Of course.
Kevin:	Be careful here. Add the last two digits of your birth year.
George:	Digits? What are digits?
Kevin:	They're single numbers, like 1, 2, 3, 4.
George:	So 13 isn't a digit?
Kevin:	No. 1 is, and 3 is, but not 13.
George:	OK. I see what to add. Not 19. Just the last two numbers.
Kevin:	Right.
George:	Are we almost done?
Kevin:	Be patient. Subtract 32,940.
George:	OK.
Kevin:	And?
George:	Wow! It's my birthday! How did you do that?

EXPANSION

You can figure out your friend's birthday!
If you don't believe it, here's an example. It always works.

Your friend was born in April, the 4th month.	*4*
Add 18 to that number.	*4 + 18 = 22*
Multiply it by 25.	*22 x 25 = 550*
Subtract 333.	*550 – 333 = 217*
Multiply by 8.	*217 x 8 = 1736*
Subtract 554.	*1,736 – 554 = 1182*
Divide by 2.	*1,182 ÷ 2 = 591*
Your friend adds her birth date (27th).	*591 + 27 = 618*
Multiply by 5.	*618 x 5 = 3,090*
Add 692.	*3,090 + 692 = 3,782*
Multiply by 20.	*3,782 x 20 = 75,640*
Your friend adds the last two digits of her birth year (1996).	*75,640 + 96 = 75,736*
Subtract 32,940.	*75,736 – 32,940 = 42,796*

See, it's 4/27/96; 4 = April; 27 = date; 96 (or 1996) is the year.

Let's Chat: ESL Dialogues

Language Functions

The 1997 TESOL publication *ESL Standards for Pre-K–12 Students** sets forth goals and standards that are built around a functional approach to language learning. The dialogues in this book follow such an approach. While attempting to capture the kinds of subjects and situations young students actually talk about, the dialogues also reflect the range of functions that their language contains. Most language exchanges are multifunctional; that is, they express more than one function.

The table of functions below identifies most of the central and many of the peripheral functions of the language in this book's dialogues. Students and teachers wishing to focus on a particular function may use the table to quickly identify the corresponding dialogues.

The functions listed in the table are specific to this book. For the most part, however, they fall under the following goals and standards from *TESOL'S ESL Standards for Pre-K–12 Students.*

Goal 1: To Use English to Communicate in Social Settings

Standard 1: Students will use English to participate in social interaction.

Standard 2: Students will interact in, through, and with spoken and written English for personal expression and enjoyment.

Goal 3: To Use English in Socially and Culturally Appropriate Ways

Standard 1: Students will use the appropriate language variety, register, and genre according to audience, purpose, and setting.

*TESOL. (1997). ESL Standards for Pre-K–12 Students. Alexandria, VA: Author.

LANGUAGE FUNCTIONS

The numbers in the tables are dialogue numbers.

Exchanging information	Chapter 1 Home	Chapter 2 School	Chapter 3 The Wider World	Chapter 4 Just for Fun
Asking questions	1, 7	4, 5, 7, 8, 9, 10, 11	8	
Answering questions	1, 7	5, 8, 9, 10	8	
Giving/getting information	1, 3, 4, 5	1, 2, 4, 7, 8, 9	7, 9, 10	
Recounting events	5, 6	2, 3	8	
Explaining, giving reasons	8	6, 7, 9, 10		2
Giving details	1, 7	12		
Clarifying		5	3	2
Confirming information	7		8	

Guiding and conducting action	Chapter 1 Home	Chapter 2 School	Chapter 3 The Wider World	Chapter 4 Just for Fun
Making plans	1, 11	9	3, 4, 9	
Making decisions		5	2, 3	
Extending/accepting invitations	1			
Giving directions/instructions	2, 9	5	8	4
Requesting			3, 6	
Making demands			3, 8	
Asking for help	1, 5, 9, 10, 11		1	
Offering help	4, 10		1, 5	
Giving advice	4, 8	1		
Drawing conclusions		1, 5, 11		
Exploring options	8	9		
Solving problems			6, 9	
Agreeing		10, 11		
Understanding culture		6, 11		

Let's Chat: ESL Dialogues

Expressing feelings and emotions	Chapter 1 Home	Chapter 2 School	Chapter 3 The Wider World	Chapter 4 Just for Fun
Communicating likes/dislikes		10	4	
Expressing excitement	7		8	
Expressing appreciation	9, 10		4	
Expressing frustration		3, 4, 9		
Expressing concern		6	2, 3, 7	
Expressing displeasure	3, 4, 8		8	
Empathizing	8, 11	3, 4, 8, 9	2, 9	
Reassuring, encouraging		2	1, 2	
Connecting	9, 11	3, 5, 6, 7, 8, 9, 11	2, 6, 9, 10	1, 2, 3, 4
Resisting			2, 8	
Expressing condolence	1		8	
Scolding		10		
Joking, kidding, teasing	1, 5	5, 6, 11	7	

Weaving creativity and insight	Chapter 1 Home	Chapter 2 School	Chapter 3 The Wider World	Chapter 4 Just for Fun
Telling stories	3			1, 3
Telling jokes				1, 2, 3